Bernard M. Baruch

FINANCIAL GENIUS
STATESMAN and ADVISER to PRESIDENTS

BERNARD M. BARUCH

Bernard M. Baruch

FINANCIAL GENIUS
STATESMAN and ADVISER to PRESIDENTS

By Harry Irving Shumway

With a foreword *by*
James F. Byrnes, secretary of state
And an appendix *by* Bernard M. Baruch

SPE·LABOR·LEVIS

Boston

L. C. PAGE & COMPANY
INCORPORATED
PUBLISHERS

oo/28/46 Personal, 84

27337

Foreword

IN ATOMIC POWER lies the great hope and
expectation of mankind for material happiness
never before achieved. In the United Nations we
have placed our faith for the future political security of the Nations of the world. Through the
latter we hope to secure the peace and stability for
the development of the former.

It is more than appropriate, it is a most happy
selection for us and mankind, that Bernard Mannes
Baruch should be designated by the President of
the United States as the American representative
on the United Nations Atomic Energy Commission.
The task is a challenge of unprecedented importance, and the man is of unique stature in American public life.

In his seventy-fifth year Bernard Baruch has behind him a career of that universal quality rarely
achieved since the days of the great figures of the
American Revolutionary era. He has been an in-
spiration not only to me but to generations of
American industrialists, political leaders and statesmen, and today he continues to be the elder statesman in the true sense of the word.

Bernard Baruch has contributed something to our national life that no other American of modern times has equaled. Placing the interest of his country above personal ambitions or desires, his great patriotism and wisdom have been a guiding factor of great importance to succeeding national administrations whether they have been Republican or Democratic.

Although never elected to public office, Bernard Baruch has served in key positions since the First World War when President Wilson first named him to the Advisory Commission of the Council of National Defense in 1916. His great work in mobilizing American industry in this first great struggle repeated itself when we worked together for war mobilization in the Second — and I hope the last — World War. His fact-finding report on synthetic rubber and his report on war and post-war adjustment policies are but two of his many additional contributions during these later war years.

But it is not in the official titles and public reports that one finds his greatest contributions. It is through his informal advice and assistance, sought by and freely given to six Presidents, that his influence for the national good has been most strongly felt.

It will be a valuable aid to our people that through this book the life of this truly great Amer-

ican may become more widely known and understood in future years, for his example is one that,
if followed by others, can guide this country down
the path of true democracy in the uncertain times
ahead. To all of us he is a true American; to me he
has been a true friend.

JAMES F. BYRNES

Washington, D. C.
  April 1, 1946

Bernard M. Baruch

FINANCIAL GENIUS
STATESMAN and ADVISER to PRESIDENTS

*E*VERY BOY wants to be a pitcher or a quarterback, whether he is fitted for the assignment or not. This is something he never outgrows. He always feels diffident about holding a second place and calling in help, no matter how badly he may be doing. It is a very brave, very truthful man who speaks as did Kipling's hero regarding his humble water carrier, "You're a better man than I am, Gunga Din."

If we study the career of Bernard M. Baruch there is the constantly recurring picture, more pronounced as he grew older, of a man being called upon for help by others who just could not cope with certain situations.

Nobody likes to admit he isn't the pitcher he thought he was, or the quarterback he fancied himself. It is humiliating to confess that someone

1

else has more ability, more vision, more acumen; in short, more of what it takes. It has been very costly to the United States that, too often, 95%-smart men in power have refused to call on the 100%-smart man who stood on call, ready to be of help. This has made it hard for Mr. Baruch, because 95%-smart men are very difficult to work with and are very sensitive about whatever shortcomings they may have.

No one has to expound the foregoing. Anyone who doubts has only to turn to the newspaper files for the last thirty years — those of *The New York Times* will do — and there in black and white is the story, over and over again. Mr. Baruch has been right about so many things; and very often, a man walking very much alone. There were frequent occasions when, had he been a lesser man, he would have picked up his marbles and gone home.

Experience has taught our leaders something. Now, those who have tough nuts to crack know where the nutcracker is to be found. A man sitting on a bench in the park certainly is anything but aloof. All anyone has to do is shove one of the squirrels to one side, sit down and tell his story. It is that easy. Mr. Baruch will gravely listen, turn the matter over in his mind, and give the answer — and the answer will be good!

It is doubtful if Mr. Baruch has ever sought

credit for every bit of advice he has given. Probably a great many 95%-smart men are considered to be the authors of certain little masterpieces of wisdom, when actually B. M. B. was ghostwriting for them.

For the last seven or eight years Mr. Baruch has conducted business on the park bench, the most accessible man in history. Someone needs a little advice and seeks Mr. Baruch. If he is a mere college president or a Senator, he sits down upon the bench. If he is a President, there comes an invitation to lunch at the White House. A fanciful way to put it, nevertheless that is about the way it happens.

Mr. Baruch has said many times, "When God and the community have been so good to a man, isn't it natural that he should try to make some repayment?"

Mr. Baruch has fully repaid it. So say the farmer, the soldier, the industrial worker, the man in the street, and the other men on park benches.

One day in the late 1880's, a tall young man presented himself for physical examination preparatory to entering the Military Academy at West Point. He had passed the written examinations with plenty to spare, and one look at him implied that the physical would be a waste of time.

He was three inches over six feet, straight, and

hard as nails, and his flashing blue eyes had the glow of health and intelligence. Seldom did candidates more fitted for the college of soldiers present themselves. Moreover, this upstanding lad already had something of a reputation for fighting and aggressiveness, qualities not exactly ignored at the Point. In addition, his father had been a distinguished army surgeon in the Confederate forces during the Civil War. In short, he gave the impression of being an admirable specimen for a future general in Uncle Sam's Army.

But to the surprise of the young man, members of the medical board finally shook their heads, explaining that in spite of his excellent physique he was deaf in one ear, a condition which would keep him out of the Point. Then the young man remembered. In a college baseball game, not long before, he had banged out a long hit. He sprinted around the bases, trying to stretch a three-bagger into a homer, and arrived at the plate simultaneously with the ball. A close decision was followed by arguments and a roughhouse. In the mix-up at the plate, someone swung a bat, and it landed on the head of the home-run hitter. That blow had been the cause of the deaf ear.

And that little thing kept Bernard Mannes Baruch from the possibility of bearing the title of "General" in later years. Mr. Baruch often thought of this later on, when he was Chairman of the War Industries Board in the first World War and providing sinews of war for other men who did become generals.

Bernard Mannes Baruch was born in Camden, South Carolina, on August 19, 1870. He was the second son of Doctor Simon Baruch, who had emigrated in 1855 at the age of fifteen from Schwersenz, East Prussia, to the United States. Simon Baruch found a friend in the new country, Mannes Baum, who kept a store in Camden, and the emigrant boy was given a job in the establishment.

Simon Baruch worked hard with the difficulties of the new language and with his duties in the store, but storekeeping was not for him; there was something else on which he had his mind, and his new friend helped him to get it. Mr. Baum sent him to South Carolina Medical College and later to the Medical College of Virginia for further study.

The ink on his diploma was hardly dry when his adopted State joined the colors it had elected to raise. South Carolina was Simon Baruch's new home, these were his people, and he joined the Confederate army as a surgeon. It was a very proud young officer who donned the new uniform and buckled on the handsome sword, the two gifts presented him by that first friend, Mannes Baum.

Dr. Baruch saw a lot of hard service, and was captured three times, first at South Mountain in the Antietam campaign, next at Gettysburg, and again at Thomasville, North Carolina in the last month of the war. It was a post-graduate course, in a way, because the young surgeon became an expert on the treatment of gunshot and bayonet wounds, with the battlefield as his laboratory. From his experiences he wrote a paper on the subject, which was a standard work for many years.

The War over, Dr. Baruch settled down in Camden and took up normal life again. Those were trying days for everyone in the South. There was plenty of practice for the young physician, but little money. He married a charming girl, Belle Wolfe, daughter of a planter. Money, he felt sure, would come when conditions were better.

Belle Wolfe was of distinguished ancestry. Her father was a wealthy planter of Fairfield County, South Carolina, who had lost everything, including his home, in the War. Belle was a girl in her teens when the house was burned down over their heads. Her American ancestry goes back to 1690, when Isaac Rodriques Marhues, a Spanish-Portuguese Jew of education and some property, came to New York. He was a merchant and shipowner, and his descendants remained in New York until after the Revolution, in which they took part. Belle

Wolfe's branch of the family then settled in South Carolina, sometime prior to 1800. On one side of the house, Bernard Baruch is descended from a family which had lived in America for nine generations, and on the other side, his father's, he is the son of an immigrant.

The Baruch family remained in Camden until 1881, and here Bernard and his three brothers grew up and had their first years of schooling. These were the days of Reconstruction, when the South went through a bitter, difficult time, a period that seemed to promise no relief. A living was hard to get for everyone, and the Baruch family had to face depressing conditions like the rest. What the boy observed all around him during those humiliating days made a deep and lasting impression. It is easy to understand why Bernard Baruch became a Democrat, the brand that never changes. "Damned Yankee" and Republican were one and the same, and many Southerners must have preferred the kind that came with muskets and cannon to the later breed, armed only with carpetbags.

Bernard was the second child in the family. The middle name, Mannes, was given in honor of the man who befriended the doctor. When Bernard was about ten years old, his father decided that there would be more opportunity in a larger city, and more particularly a city in the North, so the family moved to New York.

Doctor Baruch's talent was soon recognized. He became professor of Hydrotherapy, a subject in which he had become greatly interested, at the College of Physicians, Columbia University. He specialized in this subject, and his treatments and methods were adopted at the famous spas at Saratoga. Doctor Baruch diagnosed and helped to perform the first appendicitis operation on record. Medical history gives him more credit for the origin of this operation than it does to anyone else.

The Baruch family got along. But like so many scientific men completely absorbed in their work, the Doctor was no money-maker. However, the Baruch boys attended school, and later, college. The first school Bernard attended was Public School No. 69 on 54th Street. He entered the College of the City of New York in 1884, although he had planned to go to Yale. But the New York institution was free, he could live at home, and such matters had to be considered at that time. He was a fair student, and his brain worked fast and accurately. He had the faculty of boring straight into a thing and seeing it for what it was, an ability that was even more pronounced in later years.

Bernard was no less proficient athletically, but his college did not have an eleven. This was unfortunate for him, for he was admirably suited for such a sport. However, he did excel at la crosse, boxing and baseball. In baseball he played first base, and he was an outstanding batter. His physique was splendid for boxing; he was tall, quick as a cat, strong and courageous.

Bernard once was called upon the carpet by the president of the college to explain a fistic encounter with a fellow student. It had been a good fight while it lasted, which was not long, for young Bernard knocked his opponent down the steps of the building where the impromptu affair started.

Such a thing generally meant expulsion. But Baruch had been called a name no real man can stand, and he just had to fight, whatever the cost. The president was stern and laid down the law, but young Baruch could always charm with his smile and his careful use of words, and he succeeded in this instance. Indeed, recognizing his peculiar talents, the president suggested that the college for him might be West Point, where the use of fists was not frowned upon.

From the time when he was a little boy in Camden, Bernard had realized that the business of taking care of one's self was a prime asset. If you didn't have it, you were at the mercy of other lads who were not always governed by the rule of "take someone your own size." Often he had to take a beating from bigger boys. As he grew older, he observed that it was not brute strength alone which made one the winner; there was something which governed fistic encounter, and he made up his mind to learn it. New York was just the place, he discovered, for such education, and it was not long before he was haunting the boxing centers. Wood's Gymnasium was the brightest spot, because some of the great worked out there, the incomparable Bob Fitzsimmons and Joe Choynski among the number.

By the time he was eighteen, Bernie was over six feet, three inches in height, well muscled and agile. He liked to box and enjoyed seeing the masters perform. He had everything except the killer punch, and this was not needed in his scheme of things, for he had no idea of becoming a professional.

Bernard Baruch was graduated from the College of the City of New York in 1889, and felt ready to go out into the world. His father thought there was nothing better for a man to be than a doctor. But his mother knew about the long waiting in that profession during the early years, and she was not sure she wanted this son to follow his father's profession.

Sometime before Bernard finished college, Mrs. Baruch had taken him to a well-known doctor of phrenology for the purpose of having his youthful bumps analyzed. The doctor examined him, — or rather, his head — and gave his verdict. The boy would, no doubt, make a good doctor. He would also do well at the law; but there were even more significant indications that he could do far better in business or politics.

Perhaps the doctor knew his bumps, but his subject was never entirely satisfied with the choice of career which he ultimately made. He rather regretted not having become a doctor, and, as a matter of fact, he expected to be one, up to the time he graduated from college. The last summer, he attended classes with a relative who was studying medicine and spent a great deal of time in the dissecting room.

It was a period of appraisement, of wondering, for this strapping youth of nineteen, and even then his mind must have been busy gathering facts, setting one thing against another until some decision was made. The ultimate one had at least one correct quality about it — he did pick the right locality. Actually, he landed within eight blocks of where he was later to make such an amazing financial success.

It was a business house that dealt in druggists' glassware — Whitall, Tatum & Company, on Barclay Street. The pay was three dollars a week, and the duties that of errand and office boy, of making himself useful. There proved to be little of interest in that stuffy atmosphere of glass vials, demijohns and test tubes; nothing ever happened there, and Bernard was soon convinced that nothing ever would.

*T*HE HAPPIEST part of the new life was the chance to go out on errands in that most fascinating of places, the lower end of Manhattan. Here was a maze of picturesque business activities, restaurants, street merchants, the waterfront and its dramatic array of ships offices and wharves. Here, too, were the ships, those wonderful ships that connected this country with all the others on the globe.

Bernard never tired of moving about in that noise and bustle. Best among all those interesting scenes was an activity that drew him like a magnet, that of the great banking and brokerage houses. On the windows and in the doorways were names famous all over the world, names loaded with drama.

The house of Morgan was a particularly interesting looking building. There was something about it which made it stand out from all the others. Bernard got the thrill of his young life one day when he saw the great Morgan himself, a massive figure that seemed to epitomize the scene. It was not long before the errand boy of the glassware concern knew two things: that druggists' glassware was not for him, and that a life in that financial district was!

Soon there was an opportunity. He got a job, through a friend, with a small banking concern which specialized in arbitrage; and, while the remuneration was the same as for his first job, the work was something else, something he could get his teeth into. The very fact that it was a small concern was advantageous, because he had the opportunity to learn more angles of the banking business than he ever could in a very large one, where he would be circumscribed in action. He learned much and laid the groundwork for something that would come later.

The step up came within a few months. He secured a better job and a better field with the firm of A. A. Housman & Company, brokers, with his name on the pay roll at five dollars per week. He was in!

All his life Bernard Baruch has believed in mastering a proposition as completely as possible. As in college, boxing, baseball, so it was in this new situation. Here was the fascinating world of finance which, he observed, could do so many different things for those who entered it. It could give a man the riches of Midas, or chain him to a clerk's stool at a few dollars a week.

He looked the situation over and proceeded to give it the works. He took a night-school course in law and bookkeeping, subjects he felt would be useful. Also he pored over the financial journals, statistical sheets, railroad routes and anything else that seemed pertinent to his job. Better than just knowing and remembering all this matter, he put it to good use in the office. It became the habit of those in the office to "ask Bernie" when facts were needed, rather than look them up themselves. This wouldn't have been so good, if mistakes were made, but they were never made; and young Mr. Baruch became something of a walking compendium of brokerage information.

At this time he met a man named Middleton S. Burrill, who took a great interest in him. Burrill was a lawyer and a member of a distinguished New York family. He took considerable interest in Wall Street affairs, and he was an extraordinarily skillful amateur speculator. He gave Baruch much sound advice.

There were other speculators, professionals, whom Baruch met and with whom he became acquainted. Perhaps the greatest of them all was James R. Keene. He took a fancy to the bright, ambitious young man who was asking so many sharp questions. It was a case of one shrewd mind meeting another and being drawn to it.

It was impossible for Baruch to resist the call of the ticker tape. There it was, rolling along like Ole Man River and offering fortunes to those who could comprehend its messages. Young Baruch had an idea that he could do as good a job of reading as the next one, and he began making little ten-share purchases, watching them carefully. Sometimes he would win, sometimes not.

As in his boxing days, he took a shellacking now and then. He would run up a profit of several hundred dollars, then lose it on some other deal that seemed to promise just as rosy a result. But there was, he knew, a key to it, a plan that would make these ventures average right. And he constantly studied this, trying to get the "feel" of it.

He was intelligent enough to know that the leaders he admired so much used something more than casual hunches and so-called "inside information." Hunches and inside information led to a seat on the mourner's bench and not to one on the Stock Exchange, the latter a figurative piece of furniture upon which he fully intended one day to sit.

He did not neglect his job with the brokerage firm for his ventures into the market. Quite the contrary. He became a customers' man, he learned how to sell securities to clients, and better still, he learned how to get them to become regular customers of the firm.

After being with the Housman company for a couple of years, he felt that he was worth more salary and asked for it. The officials countered with an offer of a partnership, a one-eighth interest, and Baruch accepted. The coming year proved much more profitable, and Baruch made $8000 for himself as a partner, which was more than twice as much as the salary he had asked for.

In 1898 he made a large commission for his concern by arranging the purchase of the Liggett & Myers Tobacco Company for that redoubtable figure, Thomas Fortune Ryan, who controlled the Union Tobacco Company and wanted the other in his collection, as did also the American Tobacco Company. Baruch by then had a bigger interest in his own firm, and his share of the deal was $50,000. With this he bought the long-coveted seat on the Stock Exchange.

The deal pleased the great Ryan, who gave Baruch another commission in the same general tobacco battle, and again he filled the bill. After the smoke had cleared, everybody was happy, especially young Mr. Bernard Baruch. Now he seemed well out of the woods, and he paid back the money he had borrowed from his father to swing his various deals.

However, sometimes "out of the woods" means just a temporary opening, and, not long after, Baruch found himself back in the shadows again. For once playing the market without his usual thorough preparation and study, he went broke on a distillery stock. This was not the only time he had had or was to have reverses. Once he said, "I've had some losses that would make an ordinary man go out and shoot himself."

It was not long before he started uphill again. In 1901, he figured that there was a green light in selling Amalgamated Copper short, and against the advice of some of the really wise men of Wall Street, he began his campaign. There were some anxious times and bad days while this was going on. There were even reports that a few of the big shots meant to take him for a financial ride, but when the excitement was over, Baruch was out in front, and to the tune of something like $700,000. The stock had gone down from 130 to something around 33, and this time the woods really were behind him! However, not long afterward he made a million and a half on a railroad deal.

Wall Street was good; there certainly was "gold in them thar hills." Another chore for the Guggenheim Brothers worked out just as happily. The

Guggenheims were in a spot on a smelting proposition; they owned the American Smelting & Refining Company and the Rockefeller interests had the Federal Mining & Smelting Company. Each of these houses wanted to acquire two other similar concerns, and the Guggenheims commissioned Baruch to get it for them. This he did, and the resulting profit was large.

Baruch, the Lone Eagle of the Street, definitely had arrived. In the opinion of the hardheaded men of the greatest financial center in the world, Baruch was a speculator of the first run. Keene, who certainly knew whereof he spoke, stated that Baruch was the smartest trader of his time.

Some attributed Baruch's amazing success to luck. This is sheer nonsense because, while luck bobbed up now and then, it was pure, unadulterated genius plus great application that enabled him to start with a shoestring and run it up to the fabulous amount he did in such a short time.

Observers would analyze what he had done in a certain performance, study the tactics and moves until they thought they had discovered the formula, and then come to the conclusion that it was all perfectly simple. Later, Baruch would be accused many times of being an apostle of the obvious, of making reports that called forth the criticism, "Why, that's perfectly obvious — as simple as two and two make four." But strangely enough, nobody else ever thought of it first. It was Baruch who worked it out, obvious or not, and put it into operation.

As for these speculative diagnoses, while they may have seemed obvious, like slow movies of a football game run off for the benefit of the team, a study of them availed little. The next campaign would prove to be entirely different, and the tactics to be pursued to be suited only to that particular one. It must be admitted that the critics missed the general recipe: "Take the obvious, add a cupful of brains, a generous pinch of imagination, a bucketful of courage and daring, stir well and bring it to a boil!"

An example of how Baruch, and he alone, read the signs correctly, (the title "Lone Eagle" meant more than just working by himself), is shown in the famous "leak" inquiry by Congress during World War I.

Baruch's name was mentioned among the group of financial men who had amassed fortunes at just that time, and an inquiry was undertaken. Baruch willingly appeared at the inquisition. He testified frankly that he had made more than half a million dollars on the short side of the market when the peace note was published, but denied that he had had foreknowledge that the note was forthcoming.

An evidence of Baruch's amazing financial acumen was displayed when he testified before the Rules Committee as to why he had begun his short-selling operations almost a week before the President's peace note was made public. The single word "but" included in a cabled speech of Lloyd George's meant nothing to Wall Street or to the country as it came off the ticker, but it had much to do with Baruch's success during the few days which followed, inasmuch as the "but" in the interview caused him to believe that the way was being left open for peace negotiations.

"The thing that affected the market," Baruch explained to the Congressional investigators listening with rapt attention, "was the von Bethmann-Hollweg peace offer. That was followed by the Lloyd George speech, which gave the opening for peace negotiations. It was natural, after these, that men's minds would be turned towards the possibility of peace and its effects.

"Lloyd George's speech was notice that the door was not closed. Seeing this, I sold the market short on Tuesday before the speech was made, and during the speech, particularly when he said the word 'but.'"

By the time he was thirty, Bernard Baruch was a millionaire, a state of affairs which could hardly have happened had he elected to follow medicine or a military career via West Point. Something else did happen, however, which would have been unlikely in those other two choices — he became dissatisfied with what he was doing and considered trying another career, possibly the law. He disliked the name "speculator" and the other one that was more popularly used, "gambler."

There was a long period of this dissatisfaction, which in no way affected his ability to make money, for by the time he was thirty-two he had made over three million dollars. He once described his attitude on his early activities and association in the following manner: "When I first went down to the Street, I was taught to respect certain great minds of those days. I found they were a pretty shallow set; in fact, I found there were as many overrated men in Wall Street as in any other street in the world. So I borrowed a motto from a prize fighter of the time, the great Fitzsimmons, 'The bigger they come, the harder they fall.' Thereafter I did nicely."

Many people have wished they knew the Baruch formula for playing the stock market. To begin with, Mr. Baruch says that he remembers but one amateur — only one — who ever made a real success in the market. It can be gathered from his statements and writings on Speculation that there are certain courses which one must follow if he wishes to succeed in the difficult and exacting career of the speculator. Advice suitable to the times and the occasion was given from time to time by Baruch when he was active in the market.

We already know about Baruch's method of thorough investigation of any stock before buying, in order to learn all the facts about the company — not rumors or gossip, but *facts*. Granted one has the facts, the next thing is the ability to read those facts correctly, to pick out the one or two salient ones, which may be those that indicate which way the stock is likely to go. Facts are like a piece of sheet music. The notes may be faultless, but you do have to know how to play them in order to get a satisfactory tune.

There must be plenty of cash on hand, not only for one's protection, but to use as the situation develops. Equally important is the time one can devote to it. Successful speculation cannot be done in spare time, or in hit-or-miss fashion. You must stick with it.

In the popular belief, speculation comprises a darkly guarded but essentially simple bag of tricks, enabling one to buy near the bottom, sell near the top, and thus attain an easy and affluent life. Mr. Baruch has said that never in any market movement has he bought a share of stock at the bottom and sold at the top.

Speculation is not an easy way to make money. It means a hard and lonely life. A successful career of speculation presupposes an intuitive understanding of the ever-changing pattern of economic, scientific, social and political conditions, of the market, of market technique and of human psychology, both individually and in the mass. General Robert E. Lee won battles by studying the temperaments of the leaders opposing him. He would predict their movements by putting himself in their shoes. A speculator must plan in a similar manner, and he should be right at least half the time.

Moreover, a speculator must be capable of instantaneous, intensive and accurate study of a subject hitherto strange to him, able to sift a few significant facts from a labyrinth of complex and contradictory detail, and to act upon those facts. He must be capable of the greatest personal discipline, freeing himself from the trammels of every emotion, leaving the brain cold, clear, searching, ready to act. He must take searing losses without a murmur. Nor can he permit success to impair his judgment. Success destroys as many speculators as does adversity.

The essence of profitable speculation is the ability to pick out the important facts, to plan for the future, and then to act before that future arrives and before the other fellow acts. The man who can do this and be right five times out of ten should make money, because if he is good enough to be right half of the time, he will know how to cut his losses when he is wrong. The man who can be right six times out of ten should make considerable money. A man who has learned to cut his losses can break even if he is right two or three times out of ten.

Tips and inside information have ruined more people in the market than all other factors combined.

No sane professional trader figures on selling at the top. When the market is going down and has reached the point where one can buy really advantageously, it usually is only the experienced mind that can look through the fog that surrounds prices. It takes courage to hold on and wait for the turn, because, since no one except by a rare stroke of luck buys at the bottom, prices will go even lower for a while.

The man who wins is the man who can exercise the common sense and courage to sell in the face of the madness and delusions that have gripped the crowd, and when prices are soaring up, up, beyond anything justified by value. The resistance offered to buying and selling at the right time is purely psychological. When securities are low and should be bought, the supply is plentiful. When they are high and should be sold, the market for selling is always there.

The opportunity to make money, big money, in the market is not dead, according to Mr. Baruch. Great fortunes have been made in very recent days.

Up to the coming of World War I, the life of Bernard Baruch was simply that of a man remarkably successful in the building of a great fortune. His active career in Wall Street stretched from about 1895 to 1917. He was a member of the Stock Exchange for twenty years, from 1897 to 1917. He then resigned, because he felt that he should do so when he entered official life.

The early part of his career was concerned principally with speculation; the latter part with industrial development. The latter is a side of his business life that is little known, because Baruch during his active days was never a member of a board of directors, never an officer of a company, never even of any of the companies which he controlled or owned outright, like Texas Gulf Sulphur. He would never serve on a board of directors, although he was asked many times to do so, because he was still in the speculative field, and he believed that a speculator had no business being on a board.

The large industrial undertakings in which he was a big factor were Texas Gulf Sulphur, Utah Copper, Intercontinental Rubber Company, and Alaska Juneau Gold Mining Company. All of these were pioneering efforts. Texas Gulf Sulphur enabled the United States to retain control of the world sulphur market. The Utah Copper Company, by the development of the Jackling process for mining porphyry low grade rock, doubled the world output of copper. Intercontinental Rubber showed that rubber could be made from the guayule plant. It was the beginning of a development which Baruch believed and still believes would enable American manufacturers to grow their own rubber in Mexico and in parts of the United States. Alaska Juneau was a pioneering effort which achieved success in that gold was profitably extracted for the first time from ore running 80 cents to the ton, by a process that would have been called madness a few years before.

*T*HERE HAVE been several milestones in Bernard Baruch's progress, but there is little doubt that the most significant one was his meeting with Woodrow Wilson, to whom he was introduced by William McCombs, a co-trustee of the College of the City of New York. Once he had talked with the future War President, Baruch declared that he had met one of the few great men of the world.

Baruch, as has been noted, was a staunch Democrat and had always given generously to campaign chests. When Woodrow Wilson was nominated for the Presidency, Baruch contributed even more generously. It was inevitable that the two should meet, and when they did, there began a friendship and mutual admiration that was to endure without a break.

From the start, Wilson sought the advice and counsel of this new friend, especially in those fields in which Baruch was so well informed. It was pleasant for the latter to find himself in a new life, meeting a different class of men than he had known in the Street. Perhaps he did not remember the words of the old phrenologist who had said so many years before that he would succeed best in business or politics. If he did remember those words, they must have seemed prophetic. At any rate, the new life was even more exciting than the old, and Baruch began to take frequent trips to Washington.

He held no office, was appointed to no committee for four years, but that interlude gave him the opportunity to learn the intricate ways and byways of Washington. The time was soon coming when he would make good use not only of what he had learned in the Capitol, but of all that miscellaneous knowledge he had gathered as a student of industry, and — which made him immensely proud and happy — for the good of his country.

In the late summer of 1916, we were not in the war, but everything pointed to our eventual inclusion. In August, Congress established the Council of National Defense, and President Wilson appointed Bernard Baruch a member of the advisory commission. As we drew nearer to war, this body proved inadequate for the big task; and in March, 1918, the War Industries Board was created, with Bernard Baruch as Chairman. President Wilson had been sounding out Baruch for five years and knew he had the right man for one of the most difficult jobs of the war. When Baruch was given the portfolio, it was explained that he was to be the "General Eye" of the movement. Newspapermen quickly shortened "General Eye" to "General I." The President, for obvious reasons, often called Baruch "Dr. Facts."

Baruch's house was in order. He liquidated his market holdings and put $5,000,000 into Liberty bonds. His taxable income dropped from its prewar $2,300,000 to $617,000 in 1917, and he took a loss for 1918. He was not connected with any business and had sold his seat on the Exchange.

It was a tremendous undertaking, this new job, but existing conditions were bad. To put it briefly, things were a mess. This great Board took autocratic control over every industry in America. It had to function not only for us but for the Allies as well. It had to keep things regulated and keep them moving in the right direction with all possible speed. Other wars had been fought with the horrible spectacle of thousands of soldiers sent to their deaths through the inefficiency of home officials. It was up to Mr. Baruch and his War Industries Board to see that this did not happen again.

Red tape was given short shrift. Anything incompetent that got in the way, human or otherwise, was removed. A big book could and ought to be written about some of Baruch's exploits while running the WIB. There was the time, for example, when President Wilson told him that the United States must acquire all Austrian shipping in American ports. The surprised President got a telephone call the following morning from his Chairman: "The Austrian shipping has been purchased, Mr. President." And there was the time when the French Ambassador put in a frantic call to America for gasoline. Baruch had two tank steamers of gasoline on their way to France in forty-eight hours.

He hired an entire floor of a big office building

for himself and staff. One of his secretaries explained that they needed more space, but no more rooms were to be had. "All right, buy the building," ordered Mr. Baruch. He spared neither himself nor his fortune. At one time, he paid out of his own pocket the expenses of a mission to Europe to study the distribution of materials sent across the ocean. He also put up money to establish a hospital for the workers of the Board during the flu epidemic.

His first job was to provide raw materials. With a speculator's foresight, he bought up a supply of toluol (for TNT) before the army was fully aware of its importance. By adroit bluffing, he got the Chilean Government to help knock the price of nitrates from 7½ cents to 4⅛ cents a pound. He got jute from India at his price by threatening to withhold the silver shipments that stabilized India's rupee. Through Vance McCormack, he got iron from Sweden and wangled mules from Spain.

In effect, Baruch invented modern economic warfare. There is no knowing how much money was saved for the United States Government by Baruch's shrewd trading, but there is no doubt the figures would total a generous several hundred million dollars.

Baruch's master blueprint for industrial mobilization brought order out of the war's early confusion. As all-powerful Chairman of the WIB, he established the first wartime priorities system for materials and labor, set up production schedules and cut down civilian industries.

What Baruch did as head of the WIB is well-known. For once, soldiers were not neglected at the front. The speed in operations surprised everyone, especially the Germans and the German generals, who wrote glowingly, if grudgingly, about it in their memoirs.

After the end of the war came the Peace Conference at Paris. President Wilson went over, and later Baruch followed as adviser. That great gathering in Paris made history, and Mr. Baruch saw it made. He thought it was a mistake to bear down too hard on Germany, not because of too kindly feelings towards the Germans, but because it was not good business. He argued that an entirely crushed nation hardly could be expected to make good on reparations, that half a loaf was better than none. He felt that a too heavy foot on Germany's neck meant all liabilities and no assets. He thought, too, that the United States ought to have some security or guarantee for the great war debts, and this did not increase his popularity with the Allied diplomats, who were out for bargains. But the great war President trusted and depended upon his adviser. And later, when Mr.

Wilson was stricken and lay ill in bed for months, Baruch was one of the very few who were allowed to see him. Their friendship ended only with the President's death.

*T*HE END of the war saw a great letdown both to soldiers and to those who had worked as closely with them as had Bernard Baruch. It was difficult to see things in the old way. Speculation in the greatest market in the world now seemed flat. Baruch had been in public life, had moved in a larger sphere of action, and now had no desire to tie himself to a ticker again. There was as much to do as before, and more time in which to do it. He still wanted to help.

His interest centered in the great question of agriculture and the vast army of men engaged in it. These men needed help, and he meant to give it to them. After the Administration changed hands, he had no office with sweeping powers, but he did have a knowledge of how to get things done and a force of men who liked to work with him. In spite of his connection with Wall Street, the farmers liked and trusted him.

He gave a great deal of time and effort to the case of the tobacco growers. He worked out a campaign to take surplus crops off their hands and thus saved them from a bad situation. He was appealed to by the Kansas State Board of Agriculture, and again he answered with a plan which was not only successful in solving their problem, but which helped in other parts of the country. For these efforts and many others in the farmers' behalf, he charged no fee.

Baruch did not reopen his offices for ten years after the war was over. The new interests took him all over the country, and an office was superfluous.

Farmers were not the only ones who availed themselves of his uncanny wisdom. He was a Democrat, but the Republican Presidents were not above asking his advice from time to time.

Bernard Baruch has always kept himself in fine physical trim. An amusing incident pertains to his stay in Washington in wartime. One day, while walking out of a restaurant, he was imprisoned in a revolving door opening on the street by three young college men who thought of having some fun with him. They kept the dignified official trotting swiftly around with the door for several minutes. Finally they released him.

Baruch was angry and began to lecture one of the youths, who looked like a football player, and who had been drinking. The husky youth bristled and growled, "You needn't get sore. If you're looking for trouble, you can have it."

Things looked like a scrap for a minute, but just then a bystander who had known Mr. Baruch for years, stepped up to the young belligerent and whispered, "Young fellow, you'd better let that grayhaired man alone. He's got a punch like the kick of a mule. I saw him hit a man so hard once he almost changed his religion!"

The young man noted the glitter in the Baruch eyes and also his powerful, athletic build and decided to take the advice. He walked away, muttering.

Baruch had made a sizable fortune, and after the war years, decided to enjoy it. He had no inclination to spend all his life piling up dollars. He had bought a huge holding in South Carolina, and to this he often went for rest, hunting and fishing. This country estate of 16,000 acres is called "Hobcaw Barony" and is located in the Georgetown coastal region. There are within its boundaries islands, rice fields, timberlands, pine woods and marshes — a diversified and beautiful sweep of territory. The first owner of Hobcaw was Lord Carteret, who obtained it as a royal grant. Later, the Huger family held it for generations, but after the Civil War, it passed out of their hands. Mr. Baruch bought it up piece by piece until he got it all together again.

President Wilson had offered Bernard Baruch

the post of Secretary of the Treasury, but the offer had been declined. Mr. Baruch once said, as he discussed his life, "I've had a full and varied life. If my call should come tomorrow, I'd have nothing to complain about. During my younger days in Wall Street, I had contact with the older financiers and with the great railroad barons, the ferocious, cigar-chewing men who drove back the frontier with every blow on a spike. Then, years later, I was in Washington during the most stirring period of the War. After that, I went to Paris and saw the statesmen of a dozen flags sew the map of Europe into something that they hoped would hold together. All this came to me before I was forty-eight. Yes, I've had a vivid life, and I've no reason to envy any man."

Speculator Baruch had not changed his spots, if we use the word speculator as "one who observes and then acts accordingly." He did not make the universal mistake of taking an armistice for a guarantee that nobody would ever want to fight again. He knew very well that somebody would, and also he knew his own countrymen — nice people, but inclined to be careless. Early in the 1920's, seeing the trend of opinion, he became alarmed and began working on a plan to insure safety to the United States, just in case. He came out definitely for military strength, constant military strength.

Perhaps his early experiences as a boxer had something to do with this. Any man with this experience knows that it is that ever-present power, the big fist, that keeps one vertical in the ring. Also, Baruch knew, better than any other man, that preparedness in industry is no less vital than the well-trained, well-equipped army. There were other points to the plan that he preached wherever he could get a hearing, such as Government control of prices. In short, it was a plan by an acknowledged expert to have the United States always ready and competent to wage war as the best insurance against war.

He did have a little success. At least he got a hearing, and some Congressional action was taken. But everyone is now aware of what went on during the Silly Twenties. We were too big, war was unthinkable, and it was old-fashioned, anyhow. It was more fun to make money and to spend it, and there was Santa Claus, or some other handy Saint, who would always take care of us. Battleships were scrapped, and songs were written about Mother not wanting her boy to be a soldier. For the ensuing dozen years, it all headed up beautifully to extremely good news for a brooding character with a heavy bang of hair over one eye and a Charlie Chaplin moustache, over in Europe.

There were a few lone individuals in this age

who really knew what was taking place, not the least of them being the neglected and badly treated General Billy Mitchell. Bernard Baruch really did know the answers, and if we had only taken his advice and acted upon it, the whole course of events might have been changed. Japan, we learn, made mistakes, but she never made passes while looking down the muzzle of a big gun!

It may be that the election of a Republican President started Bernard Baruch on his unique career of Adviser Without Portfolio, or at least crystallized the nature of it. Before the change in Administration, he had been Woodrow Wilson's friend, an ardent Democrat. It was not to be supposed that Warren G. Harding would need the use of any ardent Democratic brains, since Republicans have never been exactly backward in admitting they possessed a few of their own. But President Harding did listen to advice from Mr. Baruch and was glad to get it.

So did the two following Republican Presidents, Coolidge and Hoover. All through the twelve Republican years, Bernard Baruch offered his services as adviser to the Administration, and in many instances, his counsel was accepted. Baruch had no office, no title, yet his influence in the national scene was considerable.

There was a time when Baruch toyed with the

idea of becoming the publisher of a big daily newspaper. He could have bought one, and this would have been a powerful agent in putting through the measures that he planned, in voicing the ideas that seemed to him so vital. But he finally decided against this exacting life, feeling that he could carry on best in the way he had started.

When the Democratic Party took over in 1932, one would suppose that about the first man to call on for help (and did they need it!) was Bernard Baruch. Indeed, there has always been considerable wonder why he was not given as important a job in the economic field then as he had had in World War I with industry. Certainly, if we remember the picture in the early 1930's, there was need of a man who knew that two and two make four, a mathematical equation in which Bernard Baruch is considered an expert.

There were dark days in the beginning, and if there was a rainbow in the sky, only the crackpots seemed to know where it was. Whatever history may say about the doings of the strange young men in Washington in those days, life was anything but dull.

Some say Bernard Baruch was a Brain Truster and one of the best, at that. A political writer took an opposite view and called him a "Fallen Angel" and a "Hitchhiker on the New Deal Band Wagon."

Regardless of his standing, it is fortunate for the country that Baruch was in there pitching, advising, appearing before committees, writing, using his influence with his many friends in Washington in matters he thought right. As we look back on all that he said and advised, it looks as if he was a right handy man to have around. Of course, we know it *now*, but then it was different. If anyone doubts this, he has only to read what Mr. Baruch advised on the subjects of industry in war, of stockpiling rubber, tin and other vital commodities, of a big well-trained army, of price control, and measures against inflation.

With so large an experience in the business of running an important part of a war, plus what he had seen at the Peace Negotiations, plus what he had observed on his annual visits to Europe, it is no wonder that he began urging a better state of mind and preparedness for his peculiarly naive countrymen. All around him was complacency, a thousand aims and pursuits, with the one important thing ignored — suitable preparation for trouble in case it did come.

In a sense, Baruch never did lay down his job with the War Industries Board. As early as 1934, he began preaching for a suitable stockpile of two exceedingly important items, rubber and tin. As the European war debts were not being taken to heart save by conscientious Finland, Baruch suggested that we get these two items from debtor countries as part payment for the debt. And that will do for a good example of shrewd trading until a better one comes along! However, the pigeon-holes got this one, too.

*I*N *1935* came another milestone in Baruch's life. He had nothing to do with starting it, but he most certainly finished it. For some time, Baruch had been under fire from critics, notably Father Coughlin and the late Senator Huey Long, the accusations seeming to convey the idea that he had cleaned up on war stocks, that there was more than a patriotic interest in his ardent campaign for preparedness.

The thing began to boil during the hearings before the Nye Senate Committee on Investigation of the Munitions Industry. It is not difficult to recall some of the accusations that came over the radio about the terrible Mr. Baruch, the sins of the International bankers (whoever they may be) and all the other stuff so dear to the heart of the rabble-rouser.

Baruch appeared before that Senate Committee one day in April and spoke his piece: "As the question of my fitness to pass an opinion upon the grave social problem of war profit lies in a test of my character, and as it is evident that a test is to be made of my record during the service I gave my country, it seems to me that the course to follow is to plunge at once into that subject, so that you may either put an end to the insinuations and innuendoes, the existence of which I would be childish to deny; or that you find me guilty of violation of the trust and confidence imposed upon me during that period.

"There is no question you can ask me as to my fortune that I won't answer. I am ready to state exactly what I own and what any member of my family owns. No matter how personal the question may be, I stand ready to answer it."

Then he read a letter that he had written to Senator Nye a few days before in which he said: "In response to your letters of March 8 and of March 18 and your telegrams of March 20, copies of which and of my replies thereto are attached, I am turning over to your messenger the material relating to my income and my taxes during the years 1916 to 1919 inclusive, for which you asked.

"Immediately on learning that the Committee was interested in my personal finances during the period in question, I had a search made of all my records which might supply the data you seek. I supplemented this effort with a request made to the Bureau of Internal Revenue that copies of my tax returns in their possession be forwarded to me. Copies of my letters of March 14 and 18 to the Internal Revenue Bureau and of the reply thereto are attached.

"In that reply you will notice that the Bureau supplied photostatic copies of my income tax returns for the years 1916 and 1917, which I enclose, although an impression was somehow created that your committee was unable to get any copies of my returns. Further, the Bureau informed me that, while the original returns for 1918 and 1919 had been destroyed and my copies had not been sent back, they were supplying to me full copies of the reports made by the field agents of the Internal Revenue Commission based upon my returns for those years. My examination of them indicates that they are comprehensive and supply the basic facts as contained in the returns themselves.

"You ask me for 'a statement of the stocks and other securities held from 1916 to 1919.' In a memorandum attached I am making an effort to comply with this request, although it is not easy to do so, for it deals with accounts from sixteen to twenty years old. However, I think the list is fairly complete. It shows all those securities which I held then and hold still, mostly bonds, and it is as complete as I can make it with respect to other securities. It is based upon an old list which my secretary unearthed. I am unable to set down the precise date on which it was drawn, but to the best of my belief and that of my secretary, who has been with me for thirty-odd years, it was compiled about 1919. It shows my total worth at that time. The amount in bonds was about $8,500,000, exclusive of the three investments which I mention later and which were worth perhaps $1,300,000 additionally. Further, I probably had some cash balances, the size of which I cannot recall. If there were any changes in this list, they were due to shifting from some of my Liberty Bond holdings into state, municipal and other types.

"In an effort to aid your committee, I am summarizing the facts contained in the returns or reports covering the four years in question. They show the following: 1916 Income $2,301,028.03; 1916 Tax $261,169.91; 1917 Income $617,061.67; 1917 Tax $263,762.53; 1918 Loss; 1919 Loss.

"During the four years in question I paid taxes, apart from the Government, to Washington, to New York City, to New York State, and to South Carolina.

"You will observe that my income steadily decreased after 1916. I was called into the Government service in 1917. I therefore arranged to dispose, even at a loss when necessity arose, of all those securities affected by the War. I also sold my seat on the New York Stock Exchange, severing myself from all active business. That is why my income in 1917 shows a decline of almost seventy-five per cent from the previous year. In 1918 and 1919 I reported no taxable income, as I had sold large portions of my holdings, showing actual losses each year, and reinvested the money in Liberty Bonds. My income from them was somewhere around $200,000. My holdings in Liberty Bonds may have been as high as seventy-five per cent of my total wealth.

"Never from the moment I was called to the Government service did I have a dollar's worth of interest in any concern manufacturing munitions of war. Immediately upon my coming to Washington, although I was at first merely in an advisory capacity and not charged with procurement or executive responsibility, I divested myself of all holdings that even remotely touched upon my official activities.

"I took this step freely and at a heavy cost to my fortune. I made absolutely no purchases of securities except bonds, mostly governments. In buying these bonds I was, of course, under the necessity of selling some of the other securities I had in my box, which, as the records show, were sold at a loss. From the time I entered the service until I left in July, 1919, I was not a participant either directly or indirectly in any market transactions.

"I carried through the war three major investments in which I am still interested. They were, first, Alaska Juneau Gold Mining Company, in which I invested before the war and which for many years had no value; second, Texas Gulf Sulphur Company, in which I originally invested about twenty-five years ago and which never produced an ounce of sulphur during the entire war; and third, the Atolia Mining Company, a producer of tungsten, to which you have made previous and public reference.

"I originally invested in this mine in the year 1905 or 1906. Its potential value lay in the fact that it was the most promising tungsten development in the United States. It took several years to bring it up to profitable productivity. It went on a dividend basis several years before the war. Tungsten was used for electric lamps, contact points, steel tools, etc. It became important as an alloy before and during the war because of the absence of other alloys in American mines.

"America never fixed a price on tungsten or similar materials during the war. The Government itself never bought an ounce of tungsten. It was sold to innumerable private buyers and was never allocated by quota. It was not a direct munition of war, but its use in steel caused its price to be affected in common with almost all other commodities.

"At this point let me emphasize the fact that the U. S. War Industries Board did not fix prices, nor did its Chairman. They were made by a special committee, distinct and separate from the War Industries Board, reporting directly to the President. Neither did the Chairman of the War Industries Board make contracts. Those were made by the various departments interested.

"More than a year before America entered the war the price of tungsten had risen to as high as $100 a unit. Before the demand was stimulated it had been around $10 a unit. An endeavor was made in the early part of 1917 to bring about agreements with producers of raw materials to grant lower prices to the Government, but neither then nor later was there a department of the Government interested in tungsten. The greater part of the sale of tungsten was directly to the Allies, and the price at which it was sold was set in the London markets by the Allies. In 1917 the price of tungsten dropped below $25 a unit, induced by fear of the establishment of an international executive and due to overstimulation of world production.

"As nearly as I can recall, my income from tungsten in 1916 was around $600,000. When in 1917 I set myself the program of getting rid of all holdings even remotely affected by the war, I tried to dispose of this investment. I offered it to my associates at a price which was to be one-half the dividend it would pay during the calendar year, and they refused to buy.

"Their refusal was based on the fear that there was no ore reserve; that there was a sharp limitation on the life of the mine; and that the foreign governments, which were the chief consumers, might limit the price. There was no market whatsoever for the shares of the mine in spite of the dividends it had paid. Accordingly I was compelled to retain my holdings. I did not resort to the subterfuge of a fake transfer.

"I informed certain officials in Washington, including the President of the United States, the Secretary of War, the Attorney General, the Secretary of the Interior, and my fellow board members of this interest and also of a plan that I had devised. Because tungsten had become increasingly important as an alloy, although its use was largest by civilian industrial enterprises, I ordered the segregation of every dollar that the mine paid me and directed that all the dividends should be paid to various charities.

"After this decision from the end of 1917 to the close of the war, I made contributions approximately of $400,000 to the Red Cross, the Knights of Columbus, the Y.M.C.A., the Y.M.H.A., the Salvation Army, and other relief agencies, and also for other war purposes. In this period I had received Atolia dividends of approximately $300,000. Incidentally, the mine became practically worthless due to exhaustion of visible ore reserves, with an occasional trifling dividend since then. I still have the stock.

"I hope I have answered fully as to my personal affairs. I shall be present at the time you set — Wednesday — to answer as to any further details you may wish to go into, and, at the same time, to further the work of the Committee, which I had understood to be an investigation of the munitions industry.

"I have no request to make as to the course to be followed with reference to publicizing this communication except to ask that you be good enough to inform me of your intention in advance of action.

"With assurances to you and your fellow Senators of my esteem, I am

Respectfully,

(*Signed*) BERNARD M. BARUCH."

There are at least two striking things about this letter. It is an example of straight thinking and writing, and its honesty is evident in every line. After the reading of this letter, there was nothing for the prime movers of the committee to do. There should have been some sort of public apology, some indication from those who started the smearing tactics that they had been wrong. However, it was a great lesson for the rabble-rousers not to fire bird shot at an individual who packs atomic bombs.

Before the hearing was over, Senator James F. Byrnes appeared before the Committee and told how a certain mission was sent to Great Britain to investigate the use of material sent to the Allies during World War I. There was no provision made to pay the expenses of the party up to the last minute of sailing, so Baruch paid the sum, $85,000, out of his own pocket. Also, Mr. Baruch refused to accept reimbursement of this money.

On another occasion, explained Senator Byrnes, the Council of National Defense needed an office building for its personnel, but there was no appropriation for it, and once again Baruch paid the bill. Senator Brynes also brought to light another incident which he felt might shed a little light for this committee. When World War I ended, there were some hundreds of clerical workers left stranded in Washington, whose jobs had been terminated by the closing of the WIB. Baruch offered to pay the railroad fare home for all who needed it and many of them accepted the gift.

These were not the only times when Bernard Baruch dug down into his pocket when his country needed it. At one time, some years later, vital machinery was needed by a munitions plant to manufacture smokeless powder to the tune of about three million dollars. Baruch directed that it be ordered at once, stating that it was needed in a hurry and that he would pay for it himself if the Government did not. The much needed machinery was bought, and was paid for by Baruch. Later, he was reimbursed; but had the committee waited for an appropriation to be made, precious time would have been lost, and, in this particular instance, it would have been very serious indeed.

The foregoing episodes ended any further attempt to criticize Bernard Baruch. He should have been a rascal, according to his accusers, because he came from Wall Street; but he wasn't.

*B*ARUCH ADMITS that he has been lucky in many things, but not the least of his luck charms is the fact that he is good copy. Publicity gets him a chance to be heard, makes it imperative that those in power pay attention to him. It would be a rash officeholder of any calibre who would give Mr. Baruch the brush-off.

This is easy to understand, because when he comes out for any cause or movement, he gets nationwide publicity with no trouble. Officeholders, even Presidents, are not entirely oblivious to the opinion of the folks back home, and if it became known that good advice by an expert was being ignored by them, they would certainly hear about it some fine November day, if not sooner. There is little doubt that this has contributed to Mr. Baruch's ability to stay somewhere near the biggest chair in America.

The going has not always been easy. Baruch's lieutenants, General Hugh Johnson and George Peek, for two, bucked the New Deal head-on, and this reacted against him. Mr. Roosevelt was not one who forgave too readily, and there were times when Baruch must have felt, in getting an audience at the White House, something like a book agent trying to sell a tough set of books.

Every year, so Baruch thought, brought us nearer to trouble. Long trained at reading the "signs," he could add up a column of facts and figures, each perhaps innocuous enough, and get a total that meant only one thing — *war*. There was a chance that it could be avoided, he felt, but that chance depended upon our becoming so powerful in every department of making war that no nation would dare attack us.

As we know now, those preparations were not made, and the eventual attackers got the green light for which they were waiting. In the fall of 1938, Baruch told White House reporters frankly that the United States was unprepared to wage even a defensive war. At the end of 1938, military leaders scoffed at suggestions of armament appropriations totaling a billion dollars annually. "How," they asked, "can we spend a billion a year usefully?"

It was not long before the attack that drove us headlong into war that Mr. Baruch appeared before the House Banking and Currency Committee, where he spoke on the subject of inflation and its prevention. He said, "I do not believe in piecemeal price fixing. I think you first have to put a ceiling over the whole price structure, including wages, rents, and farm prices . . . I do not believe that you can treat price control as a separate effort. It must be intimately tied up with and move in step with all other war control: wage and rent control, priorities, conservation, commandeering, war trade, war finance, and so forth."

But again Congress did not listen to him. The younger generation of statesmen knew better than the old fogey who might have been good back in 1918 but was now old-fashioned. Baruch might have said, "When better messes are made, Congress will make them" — but he did not.

It seems now as though it would have been an utter impossibility for 140,000,000 people to be sound asleep on that fateful Sunday in December of 1941 — all, as far as we know, except one inquisitive private soldier. In the morning, we went to church or read the newspaper; in the afternoon we were plunged into the deadliest conflict in history, and, as a few realized, with precious little with which to wage it. The United States was the biggest, ripest, juiciest plum in all the world, and some twenty million pairs of highly trained hands were ready to pick it! If ever there was need of brains and luck and speed, that was the time!

We were in. As the terrible, discouraging days rolled on, and we saw our strategic points in the Pacific rubbed out, it began to dawn on even the man in the street that things had to be very different. We met rationing. We found out about those heretofore wonderful things that insulated our not-expendable cars from the ground — tires.

Now foreign affairs, preparedness, all those dry, dull topics, are never very close to the hoi polloi — but *tires?* That was a personal matter, and there was very little rubber in the country. There had been remarks about that situation in the newspapers every now and then. Who was it who was always sounding off about getting some rubber? Oh, yes! A man named Baruch. Too bad. Congress had oughta done what he told 'em — and then we, and not the Japs, would have had the rubber.

True, Baruch had spoken forcibly from time to time on the subject of rubber. He had insisted that we ought to have plenty of it, just in case. And here was the case — and no rubber. The President appointed Baruch one of a committee of three to do what could be done with a stockpile that very closely resembled Mother Hubbard's cupboard.

Baruch went at it with his co-committeemen, Karl T. Compton and James B. Conant. There were two parts to the problem, to make what we had stretch the farthest possible and to bring synthetic rubber into production as soon as possible.

The first phase was solved in the simplest sort of way, no doubt pleasing three men on a park bench while making sixty or seventy million people violently angry, with the same sort of anger that a needed dose of castor oil brings. We were told to cut down the yearly mileage; to be limited (very limited) in the use of gasoline for reasons of rubber; to drive under thirty-five miles an hour; to use recaps, and, in general, make our tires last for the duration. The story will never be written about the truly wonderful and bizarre things that were done to tires to make them last.

The report was simple, there was nothing startlingly original about it, but the plan did stretch rubber over the emergency. The synthetic part of the problem was slower to start, but it finally did roll, and the new tires began to appear on the road.

There are benches in LaFayette Park, Washington, which command a view of the White House. Some day one of these benches may have a brass plate on it which might read: "Here sat Bernard M. Baruch, expounding his views to any who cared to listen. Here, if battles were not fought, at least they may have been made of shorter duration and fewer in number."

It is not the first time in history that sages have expounded in the open air. There was another wise man who did much the same thing, that Athenians might learn to reason better and to understand their fellowmen more fully. Socrates hated enclosures, too, and thought better in the open air.

Many have wondered why Mr. Baruch took to sitting on a park bench, conducting business. Actually it just happened. It seemed that he and his associates wanted a place in which to talk, one day, and no office was available. It was a nice day, they found a spot, not on a bench, but on the

grass near one, and were busily engaged when a
newspaperman came along with a camera.

The rubber problem out of the way, Baruch was
handed another job, this time by James F. Byrnes,
Director of the Office of War Mobilization, and the
assignment this time was to straighten out the
man-power problem. The East Coast of the United
States had plenty of skilled and semi-skilled
workers; the West Coast, nearer to the Japanese
menace, was short of man-power. Workmen were
jumping their jobs everywhere in the not unrea-
sonable desire to get a bigger weekly take-home
pay check.

The situation in some of the bureaus and
agencies was not too happy; there was overlapping
of authority and consequent friction, with great
loss of time, and some of the highly placed officials
were as jealous as prima donnas and about as tem-
peramental.

Baruch wrote in accepting the job: "In taking
on this work, I am assuming that the office of War
Mobilization will be effective, and that it is to be
the final expression of the Commander in Chief,
and therefore, it will not be by-passed or side-
tracked. Justice Byrnes, if not blocked, will im-
prove things by more clearly defining the work of
each administrator and stopping all of this infernal
bickering . . ."

Baruch worked on this problem with John M. Hancock, a former associate on the War Industries Board of 1918. The report, eagerly awaited by Congress as well as by the country at large, was made public after some hazy secrecy, and then the people learned that we were really at war — all of us.

The report recommended that labor be budgeted. People knew about dollars being budgeted, that was an old story; but *men* being budgeted was something new. Also, the report advised that no contract be assigned to those sections of the country where a labor shortage existed. To prevent the dangerous hoarding of labor, it was suggested that plants be prohibited from hiring any more help than the actual need and capacity. (In far too many war plants it was no uncommon thing to have two or three men on a one-man job.) The cost-plus contracts were criticized as being responsible for labor-hoarding, and it was suggested that more attention be paid to reducing the cost of production rather than increasing the amount of profit.

The report touched upon the practice of Congressional committees of taking up too much of the precious time of war plant managers, especially those of the airplane concerns, in conferences in Washington, all of which took the over-busy producers of materials and machines away from their plants. This practice was a serious time-waster at a time when every minute counted.

*T*HE HANDWRITING on the wall during 1943 read victory for the United States, with no reservations except as to time. Consequently, many minds, both in the Government service and outside, were turned to the problem of unwinding the big machine of industry that had been wound up with such speed and excellence. It would be a bigger job than the building up.

Baruch and Hancock were assigned to make a study of this great problem, and again they turned out a thorough job, a job that had both vision and imagination. These two men had seen something like it before, but there were changes in the setup here and there which gave chances for some new pitfalls.

The report was submitted in February, 1944, seemingly in ample time, but, as events turned out, none too soon.

In brief, the Report on War and Postwar Adjustment Policies dealt with the following points:

"The All-Important Question everyone asks, be he civilian or in uniform, is 'How am I going to make a living for myself and for those dear to me, when the war is over, in a manner of my own choosing?'

"Our entire inquiry has been directed toward that question. In particular, we have been concerned with the demobilization problem of the returning serviceman and servicewoman and the civilian workers now engaged in war industries."

The recommendation was made that a new post, that of Work Director, be created in the Office of War Mobilization. The Work Director would unify the forces of the executive branch and work with Congress on the whole human side of demobilization.

The job would be to develop adequate machinery for job placement and counsel for both veterans and demobilized warworkers; plans for care of returning veterans, such as physical and occupational therapy; resumption of education for those whose schooling had been broken by the war; and vocational training for all workers.

The report stated there would be Great Opportunities: "It is our conviction that we will emerge from the war with the greatest opportunities any people ever had.

"A postwar depression is not inevitable. One half of the world will need rebuilding. Enormous demands, put aside during the war and added to prewar demands, await satisfaction. Much depends on the settlement of the peace. If it be one under which men and women can look forward with hope, not fear, there will not be enough hands to do what needs to be done."

The defeatist mood, threatening the American Way, was warned: "There has been too much loose parroting of the slogan that if individual enterprise fails to provide jobs for everyone, it must be replaced by some one of the other systems that are around. The war has been a crucible for all of the economic systems of the world, for our own, for Communism, Fascism, Nazi-ism — all the others. And the American System has outproduced the world.

"America's productive capacity can perform still another miracle in a fine and lasting peace. It will not do so if pressure groups are permitted to turn that productive capacity into a battleground for their own selfish interests or inflate ourselves out of the world market."

Speed, the report said, is our most effective attack against the two enemies which threaten in the transition and postwar period — unemployment and inflation: "The very first problem to be solved was how to get Government work out of the plants so that civilian work could come back in. This raises three questions: How are war contractors going to get the money owed them? How is Government property to be moved out physically from their plants? And, while doing that, how is the public interest to be protected?"

The report warned that if plants are choked with Government property, with work in progress, manufacturers would not have room for new equipment and materials for peacetime production. Also, if their working capital remained frozen in unpaid-for Government work, they would lack money to start up in business afresh, to buy new materials and equipment. Business would be at a standstill. So it was urged that all uncertainties about Government policy on settling terminated contracts be removed: "We recommend quick, fair and final settlement of terminated war contracts through negotiations by the contractors and the procurement agencies."

The report also pointed out that the plan proposed by the Comptroller General to review every settlement before payment would "quibble the Nation into a panic." It would mean unemployment by audit. It pointed out that fair treatment in settlements could be made in weeks as well as in years. It recommended, to guard against fraud, that full records be kept by Government negotiators in settlement cases for a period of three years. In brief, it urged speed and fairness on the part of the world's biggest paymaster in settling the bills for war work. A system of loans to fit various types of bills due was urged, the local banks and the Government co-operating.

The report stated as the One Purpose: "Perhaps this should be noted. The only purpose of contract settlement is to pay what the Government owes. Contract settlement should not be used for punishment or reward, for making better or worse the position of manufacturers, workers, or the public. Attempts to turn the settlement legislation into a bandwagon for special interests should be fought off. To the extent that the simple purpose of settlement becomes involved with other issues, passage of the legislation will be delayed. The result, should Germany collapse suddenly, might be calamitous."

In the matter of clearance of Government property from private plants, it urged a deadline of not more than sixty days — which was good news for many manufacturers who had visions of becoming custodians of war museums.

It urged: "Considerable quantities of raw materials, equipment, semifinished parts and inventories will come into the possession of the Government as a result of the termination of contracts. Prompt, effective, orderly handling of these and other Government surpluses in excess of war needs will have a most important effect on quickening

war production, combating inflation, speeding the
resumption of civilian employment as that becomes possible, and reducing the national debt,
with a consequent lowering of postwar taxes."

Also, it was recommended that a Surplus Property Administrator in the Office of War Mobilization be appointed.

One paragraph appealed particularly to the
public at large, many of whom had definite ideas
about the disposal of surplus property, having seen
some of the examples from at least a seat in the
bleachers.

It stated: "The business of all of the disposal
agencies should be conducted in a goldfish bowl,
with the facts on all sales open to public inspection
at the point of sale, and each agency submitting
reports, summarizing these sales regularly to Congress through the Surplus Administrator."

In the matter of handling contract cancellations
it urged, first, a consideration of what would im-
prove war efficiency, entailing such features as easing man-power shortages, minimizing unemployment, eliminating the least efficient producers, and
so on.

And second: "As to the second broad crite-
rion, preferences would be given to such factors
as releasing plants which can be converted most
readily to desirable peacetime production; giving

smaller enterprises an opportunity to return to
civilian production earlier, easing their termination
problems; balancing cancellations in the various
communities; reducing overswollen war communities so as to ease their ultimate return to an
inevitably slimmer peacetime level."

The report recommended the extension of the
price-control law, the priorities and allocation
powers on which the functioning of the War Production Board rests, and the requisitioning power
of the President.

There was a warning regarding pressure groups:
"Again and again we have warned of the dangers
of groups organized for selfish interests. When we
speak of pressure groups, we are not thinking
only of the individuals who lead them, but of the
men and women who make up their following.
Present leaders may go, but others will arise in
their places. The greatest danger that our Nation
faces, not only in the transition period but also in
the long-time future, is the tendency for people
to become broken up into blocs and segments,
each organized for some narrow interest of the
moment.

"The kind of peace we build will depend, as
much as any one thing, on the personal choice
every American makes, whether he or she is pulled
into such blocs or unites with the Nation as a

whole in organized self-restraint, which is the highest form of civilization."

A final word as to America: "All of the nations of the world, after the war, will be striving to raise their living standards. Without drawing upon America's productive capacity, no nation in the world will be able to do so.

"Winston Churchill has said he did not accept his portfolio in order to liquidate His Majesty's empire. No American should accept a portfolio to liquidate American living standards.

"Our great wealth can be used or abused. We have no fear that it will not be used for the advantage of America and the world in the most rational and enlightened manner. The living standards of the world must be lifted, and ours go higher — not our standards be dragged down to those of others."

Naturally a report with such scope and definiteness raised some heckles, as the authors probably expected. But as usual with the carping critics of Mr. Baruch's endeavors, they carped and then went on to other fields where there were more vulnerable targets. Mr Baruch did not reply to his critics. His reports have been somewhat like the effective sermons preached by an old colored parson, who, when asked about his success, replied; "First I tells 'em what I is gwine to tell 'em; then

I tells 'em; an' finally I tells 'em what I has done tol' 'em."

All in all, it was a masterly job, and it drew forth praise from Director James F. Byrnes, who said in a speech that the report went far to dispel the fog of controversy which had hung over the discussions of the termination of war contracts and the disposition of surplus property.

In 1944, Baruch added another gift to his already long string, this time setting aside $1,000,000 for the establishing of a research foundation for physical medicine, especially for war veterans. The plan would devote its research to the fields of massage, water, heat, light, cold, electricity, occupational pursuits, exercise, and allied treatments. The gift was made in honor of the donor's father, Dr. Simon Baruch, who, as has been stated, devoted himself to hydrotherapy.

In the spring of 1945, Baruch made a flying trip to Europe to study conditions and to confer with General Eisenhower. The Germans found out about the visit and broadcast threats, adding a touch of Hollywoodian thriller by calling themselves merely the "Werewolves". Baruch was warned that if he dared set foot upon German soil, he would be assassinated. However, the park benches in Frankfort, which city he visited, seemed just as appropriate as any other places in

which to hold his conferences with the American
Military Governor. The Werewolves failed to show
up.

*I*N *JUNE, 1945,* Baruch appeared before the
Senate Committee on Military Affairs to dis-
cuss a subject which had been troubling this
country intermittently for a quarter of a century,
giving France the jitters for over a hundred years
or so, and most of the middle of Europe for a good
many centuries. Actually, the main question was
that old; but, of course, it had come to an acutely
pointed head during the last ten years. Boiled
down, it asked, "What is to be done about the German Military Menace, that huge, apparently in-
destructible cancer which has been eating at the
vitals of Europe for so long?"

Mr. Baruch said: "No more important question
ever will come before you than this one, of how
to prevent the revival of Germany's war-making
might. It is the heart of the making of the peace; it
is the heart of the keeping of the peace.

"What is done with Germany holds the key to
whether Russia, Britain, and the United States can
continue to get along. It will affect profoundly the
jobs and livelihoods of everyone, everywhere, for
none of the economic problems of the peace can

be solved except in the light of German reparations policy and the measures taken to demilitarize
Germany's traditional war economy . . . It will
not be easy, but, if not done, we face the certainty
that Germany will make a third try to conquer the
world.

"By itself, no German settlement can be enough.
If this is to be a sure peace, we must be prepared
to see the peace through with an international
organization to maintain common unity among the
Allies, with a determined preparedness, including
universal military training, with an as-long-as-it-
takes occupation of Germany, with the judicious
use of our great productive power, and a living
faith in our democracy strong enough to give the
world the moral leadership in progress toward
greater freedom and steadily rising living standards that America had stood for since its creation . . . The time has come to end piecemeal
peacemaking and to write the peace in Europe
as an entirety. In this total peacemaking America
should move forward with a positive program of
bold leadership."

He pointed out that all the ravaged countries
in Europe looked to the United States as the one
great untouched reservoir of productive resources
in the entire world. But, he added, the people of
those countries must be made to realize that we

cannot do all they ask of us and survive ourselves. They must relearn self-reliance.

In speaking on the German problem, Mr. Baruch continued: "Any effective approach to the German question, it seems to me, must begin by recognizing one inescapable fact — there is no blinking a thorough overhauling of Germany's economy, for the simple reason that there is no 'normalcy' to return to in Germany except that of warmaking. Whether one wants to be nice or harsh to Germany makes no difference. War must be displaced as Germany's chief business . . . I have not thought in terms of a hard or a soft peace. I seek a sure peace."

He urged that Germany's dominance of Europe be broken once and for all. "Her warmaking potential must be eliminated; many of her plants and factories shifted east and west to friendly countries; all other heavy industry destroyed; the Junkers' estates broken up; her exports and imports strictly controlled; German assets and business organizations all over the world rooted out."

Mr. Baruch also advised in his remarks that "this German settlement be used as a basis for a comprehensive, all-embracing agreement with Russia on the major peace problems. By tackling immediately and forthrightly the question uppermost in the Russian mind — security against Germany —

I believe we can arrive at full understanding with
the Soviets. If it is not possible, the sooner we
know it, the better."

Speaking further regarding our relations with
Russia, he said: "America's role in dealing with
Russia should be one of tolerance and fairness.
Co-operation is a two-way street. I would like to
see this simple rule laid down: What we permit
the Russians to do, they should permit us to do.
There should be a free look-see for all the United
Nations throughout Europe. The United States
should use her offices to persuade those nations
who still refuse to recognize Soviet Russia to do
so."

Mr. Baruch added that we should "develop a
positive American foreign economic policy bringing tariffs, monetary agreements, foreign credits,
cartels, and all other economic matters into a co-
herent whole which will meet this one decisive
test — how to preserve the American free-enter-
prise system in a world drifting to cartelizations of
various kinds — to statism — so we can provide
jobs for all. Shall we settle the shooting war only
to plunge into economic war?"

And finally: "We must see the peace through
with speedy ratification of the United Nations
Organization and with a determined, enduring
program of preparedness, including universal mili-

tary training, adequate stock-piles of strategic war materials, unflagging intensive research, and the many other things indicated by a modernized mobilization plan designed to convert our Nation in quickest order to the conditions of any possible war in the future."

On German assets in foreign countries, he urged: "Enemy assets in each country should be used to make restitution to nationals of that country for properties lost or damaged in enemy countries. In the United States the value of German properties taken over by Congress would be pooled, and from this fund Americans with property in Germany or her satellites would receive restitution. Anything left after these claims are met would be turned into a common pool to pay for necessary German imports, with the balance going as reparations. This will make possible deindustrializing German heavy industry, even where American or other foreign-owned plants are involved."

Relative to our relations with Russia Mr. Baruch stated: "In the absence of common policy as to the long-range fate of Germany, the Soviets are bound to question Allied moves as dictated by a desire to rebuild Germany into a buffer against Russia. In turn, the western democracies will suspect Russia of seeking to communize Germany. The Germans can be expected to resort to every imaginable trick to foment discord among the four occupying nations. They will play one nation against the others, one zone against the next, hoping to break the common unity of the Allies, so controls will be permitted to lapse, giving her a chance to recoup, as after Versailles."

Mr. Baruch pointed out that, on reviewing recent events, it was to be understood that there was considerable cause for suspicion between Russia and the western democracies. The pledged word, he said, was the best antidote to suspicion: "Above everything else, there must be the most meticulous observance on our part of all our obligations with the Soviets, written or implied, while insisting firmly that they do the same. By doing our homework before going to conferences, agreements can be free of ambiguity."

History indicates that Baruch and others at the Peace Negotiations in 1919 were too lenient with Germany. It appeared during this hearing that a lesson had been thoroughly learned. In subsequent remarks at the hearing, Mr. Baruch said: "I do not want to build up their (the Germans') machinery now; I do not want to do business with them now. I do not think they should be permitted to produce beyond what they need for their own necessities. I want to break their war machine once and for all . . . If our first object is to keep them from having another war machine, you have to do what needs to be done. You cannot let them revive industrially and become a warlike nation again . . . I have made my choice. This is the second World War I have seen, and I do not want to see a third one. In my opinion, you cannot industrialize Germany and keep her from being a war agency."

*I*N SEPTEMBER, 1945, Baruch submitted a Report on Veterans' Matters to General Omar N. Bradley, Veterans' Administrator. Mr. Baruch warned in the report that the human side of demobilization was being neglected tragically:

"Solution of the veterans' problems does not — cannot — proceed alone. During the period when our soldiers and sailors will be shedding their uniforms, six to eight million workers in strictly war industries will be shifting jobs or homes. The ultimate goal of any veterans' program must be to restore the returning soldier and sailor to the community — socially, economically, and humanly.

"This cannot be accomplished except as part of the larger program embracing the whole of human demobilization. One terrible danger of failure may be to set the veteran off from the rest of the

Nation, cherishing the grievance of having been wronged, at odds with fellow-Americans, his feelings an explosive fuel ready to be ignited by some future demagogues."

Baruch urged the immediate naming of a vigorous, imaginative Work Director to act as a single, unforgetful mind to make certain that the human side of demobilization is not forgotten. He also urged the setting up of three different committees: the first, to make an impartial study and public report, aiming at the complete transformation of the veterans' medical service; a second, to make a similar study of non-medical matters of the Veterans' Administration to simplify and decentralize its procedures; and a third, to work with Congress in making an intensive review of all existing GI (pertaining to veterans) legislation in need of amending.

Another point strongly emphasized by Baruch was the need to end the run-around being given veterans in many communities by seeing to it that in each community there would be only one place where veterans need go — in dignity and not for charity — to learn all of their rights and how to get them.

In summarizing, Mr. Baruch said: "We have here a matter in which there is no question of what our people would like to see done. What is

at question is our competence to carry out obligations which all of us recognize and wish to see
fulfilled. We must not fail the veterans — for then
we fail ourselves. We fail our Nation with its herit-
age of greatness which is the challenge to all the
world. We must show that our political and economic system, which met the test of war so mag-
nificently, can be turned as effectively to the
solution of the human problems in the return to
peace."

*I*F MEN'S MINDS had not turned toward
science by the late summer of 1945, the events
in Japan convinced the dullest that war had lost
its accent on pure brawn and courage and had
entered on a new phase. Suddenly in the names of
heroes in the public prints there appeared those
of a few professors of science, a few men unknown
to the masses and among them a woman.

The public was slow to see how a handful of
"absent-minded" professors had suddenly ended
a war. Their atomic bomb had burned out huge
sections of a few places in Japan, with the result
that a cocky nation, plentifully supplied with
trained men, had been forced to quit cold. Those
who were skeptical had only to look at the photo-
graphs of the destruction to believe. The thought-

ful woke up in a matter of hours. "If we can do it," they asked, "why can't some enemy do it to us?"

Every time men have invented a new weapon, some other men have evolved a counter weapon of some sort. Only a dullard would suppose that the Germans and Japanese are not able to think, to invent, to execute. Only one with his head buried in the sand would suppose that so many million defeated soreheads would take their defeat lying down.

There was no doubt, there is no doubt now, that science will supply some very big answers to problems of existence in the future, near and far. Washington, even holding most of the aces and face cards of the moment, became very interested, and in November, 1945, Baruch appeared before the Senate Committee on Military Affairs to give his views on Science Legislation.

He began by pointing out that all the spectacular innovations of scientific warfare — like radar, atom-bombs, and so on — had induced the public to believe that nothing but scientific advance was needed for national safety, but that such a notion invited a terrible calamity. Vital as it is, he warned, scientific research is not a substitute for universal training, or modernized, industrial mobilization.

Mr. Baruch said: "As a result of the experience in the first war, there was recommended, as part of the over-all national mobilization plan, a mobilization of the various professions — scientific, medical, engineering, chemical, electrical, mechanical and mining. This plan never was put into effect. After Hitler invaded Poland in 1939, continual suggestions were made for such a mobilization . . .

"Finally, the President created the Office of Scientific Research and Development, which brought into being many effective instrumentalities for war and peace . . .

"What should the Government aim for through a peacetime, scientific program such as this Committee contemplates? I would list eight major goals: 1. Greatly increase our scientific brainpower, using scholarships and other aids to develop new scientific talent in American youth. 2. Continued, vigilant military research in developing new weapons for national defense. 3. Intensify science's war against disease. 4. Offset the depletion of our natural resources. 5. Stimulate basic scientific research to assure a continued flow of new, fundamental, scientific knowledge. 6. The widest, most efficient spread of scientific information, both of as yet undisclosed war discoveries and future findings. 7. Create a new, permanent, Government agency to co-ordinate these many activities into an integrated, national, scientific policy. 8. This agency to provide the expert counsel for the freest, worldwide exchange of scientific knowledge and for effective policing of the war-geared science of Germany and Japan."

Baruch also recommended a national resources inventory as necessary not only to guide scientific research but to pursue intelligent, financial and economic policies, both domestic and foreign.

The veterans and their problems have been very close to Baruch's heart. This is a fact well known to many soldiers who have written him from faroff places, telling him about their troubles and asking for advice and help. He has given a great deal of time and money in their various causes.

In November, 1945, Baruch wrote to Senator Ed C. Johnson, Chairman of the Sub-Committee on Veterans' Legislation, submitting a chart comparing the legislative benefits that have been enacted for World War II veterans in six countries, Australia, Canada, Britain, New Zealand, the Union of South Africa and the United States. He had this chart prepared because no other detailed comparison of veterans' programs of various countries had been brought together. Baruch had it made, thinking it might suggest a number of helpful ideas for improving our own program.

The letter explained: "During my studies of veterans' problems, numerous questions arose as to what other nations were doing to assist their servicemen and servicewomen in readjusting to civilian life. In seeking the answers to such questions, it developed that no detailed comparison of the veterans' programs of various countries had been brought together. Accordingly, I had this chart prepared. I believe it will be of considerable interest to the American people and the Congress and that it may suggest a number of helpful ideas for improving our own program.

"For the comparison, seven major programs of veterans' benefits were chosen: discharge payments; loans and grants; unemployment benefits; reinstatement rights and employment preference; education; vocational training; medical care and benefits for the disabled. The chart is limited to these six nations because in countries once overrun by the enemy, the difficulties of inflation and physical reconstruction leave no basis for comparison.

"In the making of this chart my researchers were instructed to 'stick to presenting the facts.' They were told to avoid judgments or interpretations as to whether any particular benefits in any country were either too low — or too high. Nor was any attempt made to weigh how effectively the programs in the different nations are being administered." Briefly, the chart summarized:

1. In the main the provisions enacted by

Congress for American veterans are more liberal than comparable programs in the other countries.

2. One striking exception is in payments to veterans on discharge, the United States being lowest. Mustering-out pay in the United States is a flat sum of $300 for men with more than six months' Service, a portion of which was overseas; or $200 if more than six months' domestic Service. All other countries scale discharge payments by length of Service. In Canada and New Zealand such payments run at double our mustering-out pay.

3. The United States offers the highest scale of readjustment allowances for unemployed veterans and of pensions for the disabled; also the most generous program of hospitalization and the most liberal standards of eligibility for education and vocational training.

4. Canada, however, pays higher subsistence allowances to veterans attending school or taking vocational training. In Britain, the maximum allowance for subsistence may go higher in some instances, being scaled to the veteran's individual needs.

The chart is printed on a large single sheet and contains a surprising amount of information easily read. All monetary benefits have been translated into American dollars and cents at the Federal Reserve's certified rates of exchange as of October, 1946.

In conclusion the letter said: "It is my hope that this comparison of veterans' legislation in this country will contribute to bringing our own program into better perspective. As I have stated before, how effectively we meet the problems of the returning Soldier, Sailor, or Marine is an acid test for our Democracy. The desires of the American people are unmistakable. The test is how effectively we devise the means for carrying through what the public wants to see done."

In the minds of many, V-J Day was to usher in an era of good times, with irksome restrictions off and living as it used to be. We had been told all about the terrific demands there would be for new automobiles, electric refrigerators, radios, washing machines and all the other things we had gone without for so long. A boom just couldn't be avoided.

The United States had won a war on foreign soil, only to find a battleline on its own territory a few months later; not merely a battleline, but one that threatened to have a bulge — and bulges brought poignant memories. And the bulge in this instance was as deadly, in its way, as that of the recently well-remembered von Rundstedt. Inflation was threatened by demands for higher wages and prices.

The battlelines became definitely drawn as February of 1946 wore on. The Steel Industry wanted a raise in its ton price, of $6.00 or more. John Snyder, Reconversion Director, originally offered $4.00. He felt this was necessary, not as compensation for higher wages, but to meet increased costs even before wages were advanced. Chester Bowles, Price Administrator, considered that an increase of $2.50 a ton was all the situation deserved. President Truman had recommended an hour-wage raise increase of eighteen and one-half cents an hour without a price boost.

Washington began to hear things, among them that price control was fairly popular with consumers, and that Chester Bowles was developing into the stature of a hero among millions of small people who wanted a champion against price-gougers.

The controversy went on, and soon a crisis developed. It was then that President Truman sent for Mr. Baruch, with Secretary of State James F. Byrnes and Fred Vinson.

The days'-long struggle over wage formulas, steel and top personnel was carried on behind closed doors, but enough of the news came through one way or another to indicate the way the wind was blowing. Would the line give? Would it hold fast? Columns of news were devoted to it; the commentators had their field days.

On February 15th, the people of the United States read in their newspapers that the Government had a new wage-price policy formula, that President Truman (who had canceled a vacation to Florida) had made some changes among the personnel of his top economic ranks, and that the big steel strike was about to end. The President had to give ground in his battle against inflation.

He had permitted a moderate bulge in the "hold-the-line" order on prices in an effort to get our stalled production machinery on the move again.

It was necessary to reinstate some previously abandoned federal controls over the national economy, wages and prices, too optimistically removed after V-J Day. The personnel changes resulted in Mr. Bowles becoming head of the Office of Economic Stabilization, Paul A. Porter taking Mr. Bowles' old job, and Charles R. Denny Jr. becoming Acting Chairman of the Federal Communications Commission. The new formula: The Office of Price Administration would police price increases, and the National Wage Stabilization Board would police wage increases.

Bernard Baruch played his part in this long struggle. One commentator wrote: "Baruch was instrumental in breaking one of the stalemates in the steel strike. In this he devised a secret formula for a speedy solution and for declaring a year's moratorium on price and wage increases."

*O*N *MARCH 18th, 1946,* Bernard M. Baruch, elder statesman, assumed perhaps the most imposing task of his long career — making the atom work for peace instead of war.

Drafted by President Truman as the United States representative on the United Nations Atomic Energy Commission, Baruch announced the following team of "alternates and co-workers" who will assist him in working out the problem that may determine the future of humanity:

John Hancock, Wall Street banker who worked with Baruch on his rubber and postwar reports; Herbert Bayard Swope, publicist and journalist, who was Baruch's assistant on the War Industries Board in World War I; Ferdinand Eberstadt, New York investment banker and lawyer and former vice chairman of the wartime War Production Board; and Fred Searls, noted New York mining engineer, who was special assistant to Eberstadt on WPB, who also was special assistant on munitions for the Office of War Mobilization and Reconversion, and who is now a consultant to Secretary of State James F. Byrnes.

"The President told me I could have any assistants I wanted," said Mr. Baruch. "I asked these four to serve with me. One will be with me at every meeting of the commission, and, if I am unable to attend, I will name one of them to serve for me."

Baruch stated that the necessary scientific guidance would be given by such American scientists as James B. Conant, president of Harvard University, Doctor Vannevar Bush, who headed the war work of American scientific laboratories, and Doctor Arthur H. Compton, president of Washington University. He added that on the manufacture, consultations would be made with Maj. Gen. Leslie M. Groves, who headed the atomic bomb development project, and with those in American industry who have made successful use of atomic energy.

"I approach the subject with an open mind and will do the best I can," said Mr. Baruch in his statement. "I shall have nothing further to say at any time, other than in the report to the Security Council that will be made by ten associates and myself."

The Atomic Energy Commission was established by the United Nations General Assembly in London, in January, 1946. Creation of the commission was urged by Secretary Byrnes, who told the Assembly that it was necessary to save the world from an atomic armaments race.

*L*IFE HAS been very good indeed to Bernard Baruch. He has had health and wealth. He has had ideas and has had the supreme satisfaction of seeing many of them pan out well. He has good looks, charm. One gets the impression, on meeting him, that he is a sound man, what an old-timer would call, "all wool and a yard wide."

To the man in the street, Baruch is a "lucky guy," one who walked up to the machine and hit it for the jackpot. But one has to see him for not longer than two minutes to have a more accurate answer than that. The blue eyes that are so friendly and smiling can suddenly change to two dark, burnings slits, supercharged with amazing shrewdness and power. You have the feeling that nobody living could put anything over on him. Those piercing eyes have your own number correctly in no time at all, but their smile is too friendly to make you feel disturbed about it.

Baruch is, as anyone can see, not afraid about anything or of anybody. He is very simple and direct about whatever he does. Like this: There is a chore to do. He plans carefully how to do it. He tells no one what he is doing while he is doing it. He does it, giving it the best he's got. If the critics carp, he answers them not.

In that tall, lean frame, the sharp eyes and the determined mouth, you can see the boxer of fifty years ago, and fully agree with the late, lamented Mr. Fitzsimmons that Mr. Baruch would have gone far in the prize ring, had he wished.

Something can be gleaned from a man in his office, as it is the place where he spends a third or more of his time. Baruch's offices occupy a floor of a towering building in New York, with commanding views from all sides. From this location Mr. Baruch can look westward over crowded mid-Manhattan and Hudson River traffic into New Jersey; northward and eastward over East River shipping into the Bronx, Connecticut and Long Island; and southward over the skyscrapers of lower Manhattan and Wall Street to the great, busy harbor and the Atlantic Ocean.

Mr. Baruch's office does not impress one with rich trappings or imposing furniture. It is good, substantial, and has the appearance of being used. Books line one side of the wall. The desk is free of everything save a telephone, a calendar and a blotter. There are no toys, knickknacks or remnants of yesterday's business. Mr. Baruch is just as likely to ask you to sit on one side of it as the other, or behind it. He does not sit and glare at you like a superman. He conveys the impression that you are another human being like himself, that the business you are engaged in is the thing of the moment to both of you.

There are many books, there and in his home, but Mr. Baruch lists four as all a man needs to read: *The Bible,* Plutarch's *Lives,* Draper's *History of Intellectual Development of Europe* and *Extraordinary Popular Delusions and The Madness of Crowds* by Charles Mackay.*

Notwithstanding the well-known charm, he can be quite, quite definite. When he says "no" there are no qualifying "ers" nor "well, now, on the other hands" at all; just plain "no." There is no need to feel insulted. It is "no" because it is a fact, and facts are too precious to adulterate.

During his long career he has had a long list of nicknames and momentary titles — President-Maker, Presidential Adviser, Park-Bench Statesman, Dr. Facts, General Eye, Dr. Fixit, America's Super-Adviser, Super-President, Kingmaker and of course, the Lone Eagle of Wall Street. But "Bernie" is the one used by all his friends, old and new.

Mr. Baruch is seventy-five, and mentions it now and then. Notwithstanding, he puts in a busy day of work, whether in New York, Washington or

* Published by L. C. Page & Company, Inc., Boston.

abroad. Whatever the photographic camera says (and it is still quite kind) he moves with agility and directness, and the essence which is Bernard Baruch — spirit, application, thinking power — is just the same as ever.

He has said, "I have lived a vivid, interesting life and I have no reason to envy any man." He is one man who has loved his country and has shown that love in deeds and action.

He has a place in our history. There has not been one quite like him since we started doing business at Plymouth Rock. For twenty-nine years he has been answering to "Calling Mr. Baruch!", answering promptly, efficiently and without pay of any kind. That, as you might say, puts him in a bracket quite unique.

Much has been said about this man who has never held public office, and many have wondered why one with such talent should go unrewarded. An office would have circumscribed Bernard Baruch. He would have had to operate in a groove, to narrow himself down to a single field of action. In his chosen role, he has been free to work along lines appealing to him and those assigned to him by the Presidents. Undoubtedly he has been of far more value working this way.

Dr. Facts, General Eye, Park-Bench Statesman — not one of these names alone have fitted him without a wrinkle. He has been something of each of them. There is a very apt, very American title that would fit him well and be understood by his fellow-citizens of every age — that of Head Coach. He has been Head Coach to his country for a long, long time, and when he has retired from the arena for a well-earned rest, we shall be very lucky indeed if we can get another like him.

Appendix

The STATEMENT of BERNARD M. BARUCH
in regard to
PRICE and WAGE CONTROL

before the House Banking and Currency Committee
on March 26, 1946

Appendix

I feel honored at being requested to appear before you on the important subject of price control.

In these days of speed and emergency, it is good practice to put suggestions in a form so that "he who runs may read," and to aid the digestion of his reading I am submitting, at the outset, certain of my ideas in capsule form. Here they are:

Increase production. This is the Law and the Prophets—without it the rest of my suggestions are meaningless. So I say again: "Increase production."

Stop increasing money supply.

Stop decreasing taxes until budget is balanced.

Stop bunking the public by saying wage increases can be granted without increase in price levels.

Do not fear to increase prices or wages where necessary to get and stimulate production.

Continue price controls, subject to indicated modifications, for a year. Allow profit but no profiteering.

Avoid favoritism to any particular group.

Take care of those between the millstones—

clerks, government employees, pensioners, et al.

Make surpluses of goods in military hands available to compensate for shortages.

Stimulate founding and financing small business.

Take stock before blindly lending—make inventories of our goods, our cash, our credit before we increase the pressure on these.

*C*ut government costs, including Federal, state, county and city. In time of deflation we should spend; in time of inflation we should save.

Eliminate all strikes or lockouts for a year, but arrange that hardships are guarded against.

Set up a high court of commerce—a sort of supreme economic counsel which can decide questions involved in the above points and related subjects.

Remember that a sore or rotten spot anywhere in our system spreads and causes an illness everywhere.

Avoid an economic dictatorship. We are still a free society based on the enterprise system. Let us abolish neither without the consent of the people.

And, above all, we should keep in mind that the humanities come before the dollars. It may be trite to say it, but it should be said again and again—that our first duty runs to man before business, but we must not forget that sometimes the two are interchangeable.

Having finished with an index, I proceed to my content.

T here is nothing much I can add to the statement I made before this honorable committee on Sept. 19, 1941. What was applicable then is applicable now—with this difference. Then we were about to fight the bloodiest and most devastating war in all history. There was unanimity of purpose in the country which grew with the war's approach. Now there is a new feeling that comes because the war is over. The race of selfishness is on—each segment of society and each individual seeking an advantage over others. The shooting war may be over, but its aftermath—military, economic and spiritual—is still here. Before the peace terms are set, we are adopting a scuttle-and-run policy on all fronts, eager to get home and back to normal. Pressure groups are on the march.

On Sept. 19, 1941, I said—

"Except for human slaughter and maiming and all that goes with them, inflation is the most destructive of the consequences of war. It might double or more the cost of the war, it imposes the severest hardships on our people, and, through inevitable deflation that follows, burdens the future with a constantly increasing debt and a long period of painful and bitter readjustment destroying the confidence of people in themselves and their government, leaving them open to all the old and new isms. . . . With pay rolls soaring and shortages developing, more money bidding for less goods, the danger of an inflationary price rise is imminent. If it is not taken firmly in hand in time, it may get beyond the possibility of control."

That can be said again today. Let us stop trying to do a thing, but not do it, both at the same time. We either must suffer what inflation brings or prevent it.

I have advocated for war time an over-all price control, including wages, adjusting injustices or hardships where they exist. Price control by itself will not be effective. It must go hand in hand with a sharply defined tax program; the siphoning off of excess savings and earnings by selling government bonds to individuals instead of banks; by controlling all loans; by not favoring any one segment of society over another; by priority, licensing and allocation to the greatest needs, and above all, by increasing production.

I quote again:

"Piecemeal price fixing will not halt inflation. It allows the general price level to run wild, while dealing with a few individual prices. . . .

"As inflation occurs the prices that are fixed soon become out of date and must be adjusted upward. Irregular rises in prices destroy the relationships between various costs, requiring even greater adjustments."

So much for the past. I do not wish to appear as a prophet saying "I told you so," but rather as friend and citizen examining with you our past in order to guide our future.

The price structure is one that has grown through the years by trial and error, with the law of supply and demand, increasing transportation, finding better methods of manufacture and distribution, with each government, community and individual fitting itself into that structure. You cannot suddenly lay violent hands on it and expect it to function in the way that will give everything that is needed, nor cure all hardships and injustices. One apparently insignificant act, here or there, may change the life of a whole community and upset the lives of many far distant, just as the strike of a few will cripple a city or nation overnight by closing some function that may be as necessary as one of the vital organs of the body.

We cannot be complacent, as we are being beguiled with more money with less purchasing power. The gold dust thrown in all our eyes, by political abracadabra, only confuses, with gain to no one except temporary power to the economic magicians. We must mix brains with our brawn if we would keep our world leadership. We must steady ourselves in these emotional sweeps and keep our heads, or the ship of democracy will wallow in this sea of confusion, spring a leak and disintegrate.

Whole segments of society have lost their perspective as to the rights of others. Many have lost their capacity for indignation over their own wrongs and the wrongs inflicted upon others. Many could not make up their minds whether we were going to have inflation or deflation. The wonder to me is that things are not even worse than they are.

Before the report on War and Post-War Adjustment Policies was made in February of 1944, practically every one predicted between 9,000,000 and 15,000,000 unemployed. That prophecy proved unfounded. This kind of thinking shows how momentary emotion can affect a whole people.

This report recommended certain things of which but one was adopted—contract termination.

Another plan had to do with disposal of surplus property. If this had been worked intelligently and courageously many of the things the public wants and which are available would have been distributed and become useful. Some of the factories which we built could have been put in operation long ago. The surplus problem has been so tied up that it is not yet functioning properly.

*C*ongress has just passed a law which will enable us to sell our ships. This was delayed too long. They should be turned loose on the best terms possible to all nations that can use them for commerce or fishing. They in turn will seek out in every port of the world even small cargoes of materials that can be used, thereby affecting the national and international outlook.

A highlight recommended in the report was to put one man in charge of human demobilization for workers and returning veterans. If it had been promptly done, we would have escaped many of our present difficulties among veterans, workers and civilians.

There was advanced a plea for opening up credits for small business through the Federal Reserve but nothing definite has been done about that.

The whole world is watching us, amazed at the exhibition of a giant who cannot pull himself together even to take care of his own needs.

We reduced taxation nearly $6,000,000,000 for the purpose, it was said, of stimulating business which already had orders that it will take years to fill. At the same time that we lessened our income by $6,000,000,000, we asked for new loans. This bond issue was oversubscribed, most of it creating credits that can be turned by the Federal Reserve Bank into printed money. There lies a grave menace—money increase.

We make promises to other nations of loans for purchases generally to be made here. And if not here then in other places in the world where we compete.

On every side the Federal, state, city and county governments have rebuilding programs which will increase the demands upon an already limited supply. They can be easily postponed to a later date when they will be needed.

Then, while endeavoring to hold prices, we remove the indirect control over wages by getting rid of the Little Steel Formula (which was but a weak substitute for wage control) and grant the 18½ cent increase for steel. This will be followed by increases all along the line, no matter what anybody thinks to the contrary. Call it a bulge, but it is really a break—and a grave one. This was inflationary.

I do not blame labor for wanting to retain their standard of living. For the decrease of $6,000,-000,000 in taxes and the throwing over of the Little Steel Formula naturally made them feel they should take care of themselves. I would want my take-home pay to remain the same. The corporations and smaller income groups benefited mostly from the $6,000,000,000 tax reduction. Private owners of business, large and small, were seriously disadvantaged. And so it is with every group. And all of this must be followed by increases in pay or pension to the white collar brigade, government workers, firemen, policemen, teachers, professional people, veterans and the Army and the Navy.

And what becomes of all of the people when we expect government to pay out more if taxable

profits are squeezed? Who gets any advantage
if goods are not produced faster than wages are
advanced and money printed? We cannot call
this holding the line or just a bulge. To make the
take-home worth while, more things at lower
prices must be produced. That is up to labor more
than management. Unless each man produces
more than he receives, increases his output, there
will be less for him and all the others. Each one
will receive more money but have fewer things.

We might as well admit we have made tragic
mistakes. The race between prices and the cost of
living is going on here and all over the world. Ask
the housewife. She knows better than the econo-
mists and statisticians.

Let us now face facts. We must have full production. Without it, we cannot keep any sem-
blance of modern, civilized economy or even government. We risk inflation. We mute the voice
with which we speak for peace in the world. With
full production we can escape inflation and have
our people resume their leadership.

In my appeal for legislation, in my appearance
before this committee in 1941, I said:

> "The control of prices is essential for the
> successful conduct of our national defense, for
> avoiding social and economic aftermaths of
> war, for taking the profits out of war, for the

maintenance of morale, the stoppage of inflation and the placing of America in the domi-
nating place at the peace table. As I said before, with such great stakes we cannot afford
an ineffective program of price control. Some
persons, while admitting that everything I have
said is true, have argued that the public is not
ready for such drastic measures; that various
interests have to be pacified at the expense of
others; that the best law that can be had is a
stopgap measure with compromises, one which
while unable to prevent inflation, will keep
prices down somewhat. To them I recommend
the words of George Washington to the members of the constitutional convention. As you
know, the delegates to that convention originally were supposed merely to patch up the
Articles of Confederation. They could have
done just that and told themselves we will do
more patching later on, and on, and on. Happily, the delegates chose to be guided by
Washington's advice:

" 'It is too probable,' he told them, 'that no
plan we propose will be adopted. Perhaps another dreadful conflict is to be sustained. If,
to please the people, we offer that we ourselves
disapprove, how can we afterward defend our
work? Let us raise a standard to which the

wise and honest can repair. The event is in the hands of God.' "

And so here we are today.

The price structure is out of gear. I never favored subsidies, but they have become a part of this tottering price edifice. I would continue those now in effect. I would give no more.

For one year I would extend the present war powers, price fixing, and include wages, with the provision that no raise in prices be made without the approval of O. P. A., and no increase in wage scales without approval of the Office of Economic Stabilization.

Because of the wage increase we will be forced to raise prices, but it must be with a firm and wise hand, so as to get the necessary production. Remember, we have not the stimulus and unity that war creates. We will have to depend upon the personal initiative and profit incentive, but that does not mean profiteering. If wages are advanced the farmers will surely come along, because their costs are increased and they have a law which gives them parity, and therefore higher prices as the average price levels go up. And then the wages of our civil servants, the white collar brigade—the recipients of fixed incomes—have to be increased. And, as I say, you will have to increase pensions.

There may be wisdom in reinstating the $6,000,-000,000 tax reduction. Certainly I would continue renegotiations on war contracts. These steps might take care of excess profits.

Expenditures of the government should be cut to the bone.

The strictest allocation should be made of all money so that no loans will be granted or undertaken here by private concerns or by the Federal government, states, cities and counties, unless approved by the Treasury, which must seek the approval of the Office of War Mobilization which is in charge of production.

I am not opposed to helping foreign nations. But until production warrants it, I am opposed to lending them money or assisting them except for direct needs to make purchases when we know they cannot be made here or elsewhere. At this time that would be to increase demand. It would be cruel to hold out hopes that will not be realized. I would keep the goods necessary to prevent inflation and then allocate the balance, as they come to hand, where it would help the most.

We must stop treading this economic primrose

path. There is only one way to stop inflation, and that is to get production. What must be done later can be done now. Whatever is necessary now to do to get that production, I would do.

As every one knows, I have advocated a stricter price control and higher taxes than any one else. We have made too many makeshifts. We will either have to get back and do it right, or, having accepted the mistakes of the past, increase prices to put every one on a higher plateau. The only hope we now have is that production will then be so large inflation will be stopped.

Rising prices have been due to two things:

1. Currency inflation.
2. Great demand being made upon a limited supply. The law of supply and demand will take time to work, and it is during this period that we must have controls.

As I predicted two years ago, I see at least five or seven years of unending demand. How long that will last will depend upon the wisdom we show.

I approve of the set-up whereby Mr. Secretary Anderson has charge of production of agricultural products, with the provision that prices made by the O. P. A. should be subject to his approval.

As all other production is in charge of the Civilian Production Administration under Commodore Small, all prices for that production should meet with his approval.

There should not be any strikes or lockouts for a period of at least one year by agreement, preferably—otherwise by law. Mr. Bowles's new office can carry this out, taking care that no hardships are involved to the workers—or the employers. But they can shut down and live while the workers would starve.

Any dispute between the agencies involved must be solved without delay by the Office of War Mobilization (Mr. Snyder), to which Congress has given the power to do just that. Of course, all can appeal to the President.

*T*o those who paid little attention to the O. P. A. and used the black markets during the war, there has been added many good citizens who are just beginning that practice. If a wise course is not pursued, that practice will be extended. Prices and disrespect for law will mount, and quality of goods and respect for law will decrease.

It cannot be said too often. We must have production to save ourselves and the world. But, if a close-fisted policy squeezes every bit of profit out of industry in order that some segment of society may apparently be advantaged—the government being the sole judge of this—we will arrive at an economy with our industries nearly all nationalized without a vote of the people—an economic and social revolution of greater proportions than we now realize—one that American labor will rue as much as others.

Any type of control should be directed first toward food, clothing, civilian services, housing and transportation for every one. If you will give the American people an opportunity to function, not by fear nor yet by favor, and let every segment of society feel that it is not disfavored to the advantage of another, in a few months you will see an amazing change.

I heard much during the war of an endeavor to protect the little business man. How can he live under the present schedules? Prices must be set up not for each particular one in the business, but for a whole industry. People will not work without profits.

To the prophets of evil, I would like to say that I have faith in American institutions and the common sense of the American people. We must close our ears to those who try to turn us to Statism by

indirection. We are good-natured people who can
be pushed around, but only so much.

A final word:

Do we know what our resources are?

Do we know what our debts are?

Do we know how we stand and what we have
with which to help others as well as ourselves?

Do we know how much the others really need?

Many of our difficulties will be solved when we
get going. We can't get going by adopting political instead of economic and human methods. The
human equation is the greatest of all—the desire
to function—the desire to profit. But those desires must not run wild—they must be limited to
fairness. Let us be realistic and recognize that, at
the same time getting away from any unjust oppo-
sition to any of the factors composing our economic
body.

A ll parts of society, because of modern communications, have become so entwined that it can only
function well as a whole. Sometimes only one,
sometimes two or three, missing parts will cause
a breakdown of the whole machine or cause it to
slow down. Society cannot permit a few men—
labor, or management, or farmers, or professionals,
or politicians, or members of any group, to stop it

because of differences in ideas or practices between some parts of society. While we are setting
up machinery to stop wars between nations, we
have not solved it within our own gates.

I give you this thought:

There should be a high court of commerce set
up to which these disputes can be taken for ad-
judication in order that we may work out a program on the basis of the principles which made
this country great. If this is not done, we shall
soon find ourselves in the morass of confusion that
will bring us either to Fascism or Communism;
and that Ark of the Covenant of human liberties
and dignities, our form of government, will have
been lost.

The advance in wages can make true a wish
that we all have fathered—that is—if labor and
management so will it, more and more wealth can
be produced—more things made—so that each
can share in more and better things at lower prices.
Down that path we can safely go to the benefit of
all and the disadvantage of none.

This would result in an economy of abundance,
which should guarantee a return to free enterprise
in a year.